YORK NOTES

Selected Poems

Elizabeth Barrett Browning

Note by Paul Nye

D1343654

Longman   York Press

Paul Nye is hereby identified as author of this work in accordance with Section 77
of the Copyright, Designs and Patents Act 1988

YORK PRESS
322 Old Brompton Road, London SW5 9JH

PEARSON EDUCATION LIMITED
Edinburgh Gate, Harlow,
Essex CM20 2JE, United Kingdom
Associated companies, branches and representatives throughout the world

First published 1999

ISBN 0-582-38197-5   821·8 BRO

Designed by Vicki Pacey
Illustrated by Sarah Young
Influences diagram by G. J. Galsworthy
Phototypeset by Gem Graphics, Trenance, Mawgan Porth, Cornwall
Colour reproduction and film output by Spectrum Colour
Produced by Addison Wesley Longman China Limited, Hong Kong

Contents

PART THREE

COMMENTARY

PART FOUR

STUDY SKILLS

PART FIVE

CULTURAL CONNECTIONS

PREFACE

York Notes are designed to give you a broader perspective on works of literature studied at GCSE and equivalent levels. We have carried out extensive research into the needs of the modern literature student prior to publishing this new edition. Our research showed that no existing series fully met students' requirements. Rather than present a single authoritative approach, we have provided alternative viewpoints, empowering students to reach their own interpretations of the text. York Notes provide a close examination of the work and include biographical and historical background, summaries, glossaries, analyses of characters, themes, structure and language, cultural connections and literary terms.

If you look at the Contents page you will see the structure for the series. However, there's no need to read from the beginning to the end as you would with a novel, play, poem or short story. Use the Notes in the way that suits you. Our aim is to help you with your understanding of the work, not to dictate how you should learn.

York Notes are written by English teachers and examiners, with an expert knowledge of the subject. They show you how to succeed in coursework and examination assignments, guiding you through the text and offering practical advice. Questions and comments will extend, test and reinforce your knowledge. Attractive colour design and illustrations improve clarity and understanding, making these Notes easy to use and handy for quick reference.

York Notes are ideal for:
- Essay writing
- Exam preparation
- Class discussion

The author of these Notes is Paul Nye. He is an English graduate of Oxford University and has taught English and English Literature to GCSE and A Level in independent and state schools. He has also been a Moderator and Examiner for a major examining board.

The poems discussed in this Note are based on *The Works of Elizabeth Barrett Browning* published by The Wordsworth Poetry Library, 1994. Page references are to this particular text.

Health Warning: **This study guide will enhance your understanding, but should not replace the reading of the original text and/or study in class.**

INFLUENCES IN ELIZABETH BARRETT BROWNING'S LIFE

WRITERS:
ROMANTIC
INFLUENCES

John Keats
(1795-1821)

Lord Byron
(1788–1824)

Percy Bysshe
Shelley
(1792-1822)

William
Wordsworth
(1770-1850)

William
Cowper
(1731-1800)

Samuel Taylor
Coleridge
(1772–1834)

Sir Walter Scott
(1771-1855)

Mary Shelley
(1797-1851)

Emily Brontë
(1818-1848)

POLITICAL
INFLUENCES

Lord Shaftesbury
(1801–85)

Napoleon
Bonaparte
(1769-1821)

William
Wilberforce
(1759-1833)

Victor
Emmanuel
(1820-78)

Giuseppe
Garibaldi
(1807-82)

WRITERS:
SOCIAL
REFORMERS

Voltaire
(1694-1778)

Thomas Paine
(1737-1809)

William Blake
(1757-1827)

Mary
Wollstonecraft
(1759-97)

Thomas Carlyle
(1795-1881)

Elizabeth Gaskell
(1810–65)

Harriet
Beecher Stowe
(1811-96)

Charles Dickens
(1812-70)

Henry Mayhew
(1812-87)

John Ruskin
(1819-1900)

Jean-Jacques
Rousseau
(1712-98)

1806   1861

INTRODUCTION

HOW TO STUDY A POEM

You have bought this book because you wanted to study poetry on your own. This may supplement work done in class.

- Look at the poem. How are the lines organised? Are they in groups? Are any lines repeated? Are any of the lines shorter or longer than the others? Try to think of reasons why the poet set out the lines in this way.
- Do lots of the lines end with a comma or a full stop – or does the sense carry over on to another line? What is the effect of stopping at the end of each line?
- Read the poem out aloud (or aloud in your head). Does the poem rhyme? If so, what words rhyme? Is this important? Do some lines almost rhyme? Do some lines have rhyming words inside the line? If there is no rhyme, think about why the poet stops each line where he/she does.
- Read the poem aloud again. Think about the rhythm. Listen for the stressed words. Does the pattern of stressed and unstressed syllables create any kind of mood? Does it match the mood or subject-matter of the poem? Have some words been chosen for their sound?
- What is the poem about? Do not make up your mind too soon. Your first thoughts need to be reassessed when you reach the end. Remember that the subject-matter and the theme or idea of the poem may not be the same.
- Do any words make you stop and think? Are there interesting or unusual combinations of words? (Check the meaning of any words which puzzle you – they may have a meaning you are not familiar with.)

Elizabeth felt guilty from an early age about the profits her father's family had made from the Slave Trade.

Elizabeth Barrett was born in 1806 at Coxhoe Hall, Durham, of wealthy parents. They moved to Hope End in Hertfordshire whilst she was still a young child. She was the eldest of twelve children. As a child she was healthy and active. She was amazingly precocious, at the age of eight she was reading Ancient Greek. She first became known with *The Seraphim* (1838). Her reputation was enhanced with the publication of *Poems* (1844). She is best known for the love poems *Sonnets from the Portuguese* (1850), her verse/novel *Aurora Leigh* (1857) and *Last Poems* (1862), published after her death.

A pony accident may have triggered her later invalidism which was half real but, possibly, half imagined. Her marriage to Robert Browning transformed her – though her health remained frail throughout her life. Her father never forgave her for secretly marrying and he returned all her letters unopened. After her marriage she never saw him again.

The Brownings lived in Italy – mainly in Florence – and she became sympathetic to Italy's struggle against Austria as well as wider social and political issues at home and abroad. She was a life-long Church of England Christian.

She was a tiny person: 'I am little and like things little', she said of her miniature library.

She was much influenced in her writing by the Romantic poets.

Her chief gift was **lyrical** (see Literary Terms). Letter writing was her mainstay, both to eminent contacts and to family and friends. However, she loathed socialising and remained confined to her room for a great deal of the time until her elopement. She was, however, remarkably well informed on literary and political matters through her reading of periodicals and magazines. There is no doubt that she was interested in, and influenced by, many of the literary giants of the day such as Wordsworth, Tennyson and, of course, Robert Browning himself.

CONTEXT & SETTING

THE ROMANTIC PERIOD

The Romantic Period is a convenient expression in European literary history for the period dating from 1789, the French Revolution, to about 1830, for Romanticism was not confined merely to English literature but was Europe-wide. Elizabeth Barrett Browning (1806–61) was born towards the end of the Romantic Period.

Try reading some of the shorter poems by these poets.

There are two considered groups of Romantic poets, the first includes Blake, Wordsworth, Coleridge and Southey; the second includes Byron, Shelley and Keats. **Ironically** (see Literary Terms), some of the first group of poets outlived some of the second.

There are a large number of literary interests and themes which may be loosely labelled 'Romantic'. They are such things as:

- a concern to value feeling and emotion rather than value the capacity to reason. This is expressed in immediate emotion, intuition and self-examination.
- This leads directly to some of the topics typified by 'Romantic' literature: natural, primitive man, the 'noble savage', the peasant or outcasts from society, children and childhood memory. The last (childhood memory) may take such forms as ghosts and ghost stories, dreams, legends and myths.
- The self and introspection: this may take the form of examining and evaluating ourselves in relation to the world around us. Wordsworth's poem 'The Prelude' (written from 1798 onwards but not

published until 1850) and subtitled 'The Growth of a Poet's Mind', epitomises this.

- There was also a detailed interest in Nature as a way to reach an understanding of self. This led to a complex relationship between things, feelings and ideas, i.e., the physical, emotional and the spiritual natures of man. Landscape was frequently seen as an integral part of this.

- Imagination is an important concept for understanding Romanticism. It signals the mind's force that makes sense out of the chaos of sentiments and memories which we feel at any particular time.

There was also an idea that Romanticism linked with a breaking of 'the rules of poetry'. Wordsworth's 'Preface' to *Lyrical Ballads* (1800) is a cry against what was considered correct **poetic diction** (see Literary Terms). He defines poetry as the 'spontaneous overflow of powerful feelings'.

ITALY'S STRUGGLE FOR UNIFICATION

Garibaldi, at the forefront of the movement towards Italy's unification, was an immensely popular hero in Britain.

Living in Florence, Elizabeth Barrett Browning was intensely interested in Italy's struggles for unification. In 1848 many of the countries in Europe were trying to overthrow the stranglehold and domination of major powers such as Austria. At the Congress of Vienna in 1815 Italy had been broken up into seven states with a powerful imposition of Austrian rule. By 1848 almost all of Italy was up in arms in an attempt to regain its national identity. In the world of music and literature the 'Age of Romanticism' in Italy had been one of continuing growth. The most obvious art form was probably the Opera. Four composers were most significant: Rossini (1792–1868), Donizetti (1779–1848), Bellini (1801–35) and Verdi (1813–1901). The Italian resistance to the Austrian occupiers inspired Elizabeth Barrett Browning. She made her views very clear in such poems as *Casa Guidi Windows* and *Poems Before Congress*. These poems were seen, in her day, to be daring, provocative and innovative. Her views in these poems and elsewhere reflected developments which were part of the liberal tide of Romantic ideals which swept Europe.

CHILD LABOUR AND SLAVERY

Elizabeth Barrett Browning was deeply concerned about political and social reform in England too. She was particularly concerned about the laws that affected the poor and the virtual slave labour of women and children in factories and in the mines. She continually championed their cause and this is seen clearly in such a

Elizabeth kept up a correspondence with Harriet Beecher Stone, author of Uncle Tom's Cabin.

poem as 'The Cry of the Children'. Elizabeth Barrett Browning was increasingly aware of the growing racial problems and issues in America. Her strong views are forcibly illustrated in her poems such as 'The Runaway Slave at Pilgrim's Point' and 'A Curse for a Nation' from her *Poems Before Congress*.

She used her privileged background to good advantage by keeping herself well informed of the social and political issues of the day. This led to some of the most fervent statements in her poetic output.

World events	The poet's life

1806 1806 Born at Coxhoe Hall, Durham

1807 Britain outlaws slavery but it persists
1807 1807 Family moves to Ledbury, Herefordshire; father builds house with moorish windows and turret

1809 Tennyson born
1809

1812 Robert Browning born
1812

1814 1814 At eight, Elizabeth can read Homer in original ancient Greek

1820 1820 At thirteen, writes 'The Battle of Marathon' which father has printed

1821 Keats dies in Rome; Greece begins revolt against the Turks
1821 1821 At fifteen, when saddling her pony she falls and injures her spine; her invalid life begins

1822 Shelley drowns
1822

1824 Byron dies of fever at Missalonghi
1824

1826 1826 Publishes *An Essay of Mind and Shorter Poems*

1830 Two million black slaves in United States
1830

1832 First Reform Act extends voting rights to the middle classes
1832

1833 Slavery abolished in British Empire but it persists in southern states of America; early Factory Act frequently evaded by employers
1833 1833 Mother dies; father loses fortune; they move to Sidmouth for two years

1835 1835 Family move to 74 Gloucester Place London

1837 Accession of Queen Victoria; invention of photography
1837

1838 1838 Publishes 'The Seraphim'

1838-50 1838-50 *Poems*

1840 Birth of Thomas Hardy
1840 1840 Eldest brother drowns in Babbacombe Bay

World events		The poet's life

1842 The Mines Act - forbids women and children to work underground — **1842**

1843 — **1843** The 'Cry of the Children'

1846 Repeal of the Corn Laws — **1846** — **1846** After a short, secret courtship Elizabeth and Robert Browning marry; they travel to Italy and after a time in Pisa, settle in Florence

1847 New Factory Act limits working day for women and children to 10 hours; Charlotte Brontë, *Jane Eyre;* Emily Brontë, *Wuthering Heights* — **1847**

1848 Uprisings in Paris, Berlin, Vienna, Rome, Milan, Naples, Prague and Budapest — **1848**

1848-9 Struggle by Italian states against Austrian rule; Napoleon III comes to power in France — **1848-9**

1849 — **1849** Birth of their son 'Pen'

1850 Death of Wordsworth; Tennyson becomes Poet Laureate — **1850** — **1850** *Sonnets from the Portuguese;* considered for Poet Laureate

1851 The Great Exhibition, symbol of Victorian prosperity — **1851** — **1851** *Casa Guidi Windows*

1855 — **1855** Makes last visit to England

1856 Crimean War ends — **1856**

1857 — **1857** *Aurora Leigh*

1860 John Brown, abolitionist, hanged; defeat of Austria by France; unification of Italy completed through Garibaldi, Victor Emmanuel II and Cavour — **1860** — **1860** *Poems before Congress*

1861 Outbreak of American Civil War; Cavour dies — **1861** — **1861** Elizabeth dies in Florence

1862 — **1862** *Last Poems* published posthumously

1865 First bicycle — **1865**

PART TWO

SUMMARIES

DETAILED SUMMARIES

For convenience, the poems and glossaries are
considered in three sections:

Section 1: Poems directly prescribed for examinations

Section 2: Other significant poems

Section 3: Longer poems

SECTION 1: EXAMINATION POEMS

THE CRY OF THE CHILDREN (PAGE 231)

The poet laments the fact that children are being
expected to work like slaves in the mines and factories.
The poem is a cry for understanding and appreciation
of the vulnerable and exploited. The opening lines set
the tone of bitter indignation:

> Do you hear the children weeping, O my brothers,
> Ere the sorrow comes with years?

COMMENT   There is effective use of **rhyme** (see Literary Terms)
and repetition. Note the bitter **irony** (see Literary

Terms) in such lines as the following: 'In the country of
the free' and 'In our happy Fatherland' where we feel
the opposite is the truth.

GLOSSARY   *III.3* **hoary** white haired with age

                      IV.4 **rime** frost

                      14 **kirk-chime** tolling of the church bell

                      V.4 **cerement** grave clothes

A SEASIDE WALK (PAGE 249)

Consider why   A feeling of sadness is strong in this poem. The two do
'each was sad'.   not speak but there is an unspoken link between them
                        and the natural surroundings as they watch a fine
                        sunset.

COMMENT   Notice the poet's use of **personification** (see Literary
                Terms): the 'moon and stars' did not 'dare to tread
                about', 'the footsteps of the sun', 'Silence's impassioned
                breathings', 'Solemn-beating heart of nature'.

GLOSSARY   *I.4* **Genius** genie in a story

                      II.7 **swang** swung

LOVED ONCE (PAGE 282)

The poet suggests that the experience of lasting love is
far superior to a passing, short-lived emotion.

COMMENT   There is an effective use of the word 'once' as a variant
                refrain (see Literary Terms) to each **stanza** (see
                Literary Terms).

                The poet is **apostrophising** (see Literary Terms)
                God/Christ (stanza iii) and friends (stanzas iv to vii).

GLOSSARY   *I.2* **welladay** an exclamation of sadness

                      6-7 **leaven ... leaven** lighten ... yeast (used to make bread
                      lighter)

VI.4 **sepulchral clay** the earth of the grave

4 **deprecate** express disapproval

5 **shriven** forgiven of sins

VIII.2 **acceptive** used as an excuse

A FLOWER IN A LETTER (PAGE 286)

Think what associations this flower evokes.

The poet is in Devon, surrounded by flowers of all kinds and in abundance. But when she receives one flower grown in a pot on a city windowsill, it has far more significance than all the other flowers.

COMMENT The pressed flower is a symbol (see Literary Terms) of loss that causes the poet to consider the frailty of things but also the possible continuity of friendship. The rose brings with it associated memories (see 'A Dead Rose').

V.1 **I wis** I know

VI.3 **meeter** more suitable

VI.4 **Eastern bowers** fragrant gardens of the East

XIII.1 **Harpocrates** 'Horus the child' most often presented by the Greeks as a chubby infant

A DEAD ROSE (PAGE 293)

The poet looks at a rose she has kept in a drawer for seven years and is saddened by its fading which seems to symbolise (see Literary Terms) the passing and ravages of time. However, the rose gives hope that there may be some continuity of life through associated memories (see 'A Flower in a Letter').

COMMENT The poet apostrophises (see Literary Terms) the dead rose.

Note the fine imagery (see Literary Terms) in the metaphors (see Literary Terms) in the following lines:

The fly that 'lit upon thee,
To stretch the tendrils of its tiny feet

GLOSSARY

> *I.2* **roseate** pink
>
> *IV.2* **incarnadined** became red / scarlet

THE SLEEP (PAGE 294)

The poet meditates on a line from a psalm.

Sleep and night when the dew falls are seen as a restorative comfort to all – from the highest to the lowest. In death sleep is the eternal rest given by God.

COMMENT   Notice the hypnotic effect of the many different repetitions.

GLOSSARY

> *III.5* **blasted** become desolate
>
> *IV.4* **doleful** sad
>
> *V.3* **delved** dug
>
> *VIII.3* **mummers** actors / performers
>
> *IX.3* **bier** coffin

PROOF AND DISPROOF (PAGE 311)

Notice the ambiguities in this poem.   The woman laments. The protestations of love she had received seem hollow. Although she would like to believe in their mutual love, she remains insecure and unconvinced.

COMMENT   Notice the contrasts in the poem between: then and now, company and solitude, joy and sadness, security and insecurity, doubt and certainty, all of which reinforce the swings in feelings associated with falling in love.

GLOSSARY

> *IV.5* **violate** outrage
>
> **March … springs** this whole line is an ambiguous (see Literary Terms) play on words
>
> *IX.3* **unbelied** revealing of the truth

SONNETS FROM THE PORTUGUESE (PAGES 318–27)

This **sonnet sequence** (see Literary Terms) is regarded as one of the greatest achievements of Elizabeth Barrett Browning. The **sonnet** form usually uses one sustained **simile** or **metaphor** (see Literary Terms). This was ideally suited to Elizabeth Barrett Browning's poetic temperament and compensated for her tendency to write at too great a length elsewhere.

Her love poems were her earliest poetic achievements and remained always popular.

These are love poems, written to Robert Browning before their marriage, tracing her feelings for him. They represent much that is touching and profound in her writing.

The title *From the Portuguese* was a disguise on her part. 'Portuguese' was Robert Browning's pet name for her in honour of his great admiration for her poem 'Catarina to Camoëns' (see Section 2). Camoëns was a sixteenth-century Portuguese poet she had read in translation.

In all there are forty-four poems.

SONNET I (PAGE 318)

The last line has an unexpected reversal of meaning from what is expected (see **irony** in Literary Terms). Love has transformed the poet's past wasted years.

GLOSSARY

1 **Theocritus** a famous Roman poet (*c.*308–*c.*240BC). Remembered as a pastoral poet

sung rhymed; wrote poetry

SONNET V (PAGE 319)

The central **metaphor** (see Literary Terms) is that the glowing ashes of their love should be rekindled if their feelings are to be truly expressed.

Y

GLOSSARY

2 **Electra** in a daughter, corresponding to the Oedipus complex in a son

her sepulchral urn the container holding cremated ashes

SONNET VII (PAGE 319)

The poet expresses how love has completely changed her life.

GLOSSARY

7 **dole** sadness

8 **fain** dearly

SONNET VIII (PAGE 319)

Consider the view of self presented by the speaker. The poet feels inadequate as to what she can offer in the face of the generous love given freely to her by her loved one.

Notice how effectively colour **imagery** (see Literary Terms) is used in this poem.

GLOSSARY

1 **liberal** free

6 **largesse** generosity

SONNET X (PAGE 320)

Love has made the poet's life 'burn' more intensely.

Notice the strong **metaphor** (see Literary Terms) of fire throughout the poem: love is like fire, and no matter whether the subject is grand or humble its effects are the same.

GLOSSARY

14 **enhances** makes more valuable

SONNET XIV (PAGE 321)

This is one of the most **lyrical** of all her sonnets.

The poet hopes that their love will be something eternal that cannot merely be measured to other things by comparison. She rejects love based on 'comfort'.

GLOSSARY

1 **nought** nothing

5 **certes** certainly

8 **wrought** made / fashioned

SONNET XXVIII (PAGE 324)

Think about what the speaker is reviewing. The love written down in their letters is likely to fade as the ink fades. This is insignificant compared to the lasting force of their real emotions.

GLOSSARY

1 **mute** silent / blank

3 **tremulous** trembling

SONNET XXIX (PAGE 324)

The **metaphor** (see Literary Terms) used here is that she is like some wild vine twining round him, a tree. As such, she is so absorbed in her loved one that she feels that she needs to stand back to admire him properly. Similarly, a tree can be revealed in its full majesty when the vine is cut down.

GLOSSARY

1 **twine** twist / envelop

10 **insphere** enclose all around

SONNET XXXVIII (PAGE 326)

The poet says that their love has grown deeper and more lasting as time has passed.

GLOSSARY

4 **list** listen

9 **beyond meed** beyond what was deserved (**archaic** – see Literary Terms)

10 **chrism of love** moment of love's baptism

11 **sanctifying** making holy / making pure

SONNET XLIII (PAGE 327)

The poet states that she loves beyond words, beyond what can be expressed. In the last line there is an **ironic** (see Literary Terms) twist.

Notice how the repetition of the words 'I love thee' contribute to the emotional force of the poem.

GLOSSARY   *12* **my lost saints** the friends of childhood who have died but are still greatly valued

MY KATE (PAGE 562)

The poet laments the death of one, who though ordinary, is worthy to be remembered as a person who was, in her simple way, concerned for others and therefore valued.

COMMENT   The **pathos** (see Literary Terms) of the repeated refrain 'My Kate' adds to the **elegiac** (see Literary Terms) effect of the subject matter. However, some of the force of the poem is made awkward by such lines as: 'She made the grass greener even / here … with her grave'.

MY HEART AND I (PAGE 566)

This was published in the poems after her death. It comes over as Elizabeth Barrett Browning's own **epitaph** (see Literary Terms). In the face of the weariness of life, what matters most is to have been loved. The last **stanza** especially emphasises this idea.

COMMENT   Notice how the constant repetition reinforces the sense of tiredness. Note, too, the contrast between the colours of earlier life with the greyness of the present.

GLOSSARY   *VI.3* **crusted** encrusted with / covered with
                   VII.7 **fared** journeyed through life

A *Identify to whom or to what these lines refer.*

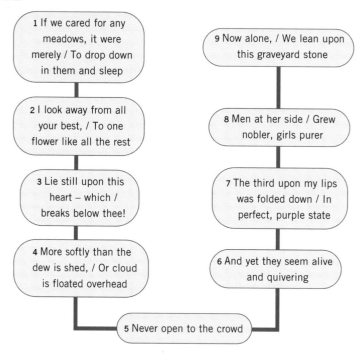

1 If we cared for any meadows, it were merely / To drop down in them and sleep

9 Now alone, / We lean upon this graveyard stone

2 I look away from all your best, / To one flower like all the rest

8 Men at her side / Grew nobler, girls purer

3 Lie still upon this heart – which / breaks below thee!

7 The third upon my lips was folded down / In perfect, purple state

4 More softly than the dew is shed, / Or cloud is floated overhead

6 And yet they seem alive and quivering

5 Never open to the crowd

Check your answers on page 56.

B *Consider these issues.*

a The links between the ideas in 'A Flower in a Letter' and 'A Dead Rose'.

b How well the sonnet form is suited to Elizabeth Barrett Browning's subject matter.

d Examine how Elizabeth Barrett Browning reveals regret in 'A Seaside Walk' and 'Loved Once'.

e In what ways 'My Heart and I' illustrates the more optimistic side of the poet's nature.

f Examine Elizabeth Barrett Browning's use of rhyme in 'My Kate' and 'My Heart and I'.

THE ROMANCE OF THE SWAN'S NEST (PAGE 214)

Think about the
ways sadness is
emphasised in this
poem.

Little Ellie dreams that 'a knight in shining armour' will come to take her away. She will send him off to do deeds of valour until he implores her to be his. She will then show him her prized secret – a swan's nest. She then discovers that the nest has been plundered by rats and that her dream is but a dream. With this, she feels bound to face the stark realities and drudgery of real life and tolerate them.

COMMENT

A 'Romance' (see Literary Terms) is a poem based on the pattern of a medieval romantic (see Literary Terms) tale. The poet uses archaic (see Literary Terms) language throughout to create the romantic atmosphere. She used this form in several other poems.

Note here the symbols (see Literary Terms) of beauty – the swan's nest, natural surroundings and dreams of romantic love. These are easily destroyed by reality – rats and destruction – and force a more realistic focusing of life.

GLOSSARY

IV.3 **steed** a fine horse

4 **without guile** genuinely

V.1 **red-roan** mottled red

IX.4 **nathless** nevertheless

XI.4 **gage** pledge

XII.2 **guerdon** reward

XIV.4 **troth** promise

XVI.3 **osier** willow tree beside a river

THE RUNAWAY SLAVE AT PILGRIM'S POINT (PAGE 228)

A slave-girl falls in love with another slave in the sugar-cane fields but he is killed. She is raped by a white man and has his child which she strangles using her shawl.

She is then flogged and dies. Her religious faith is firm despite the behaviour of the white men.

COMMENT   Although there is much that is **melodramatic** (see Literary Terms) in this poem, the slave girl's anger is very well realised.

The poem was written in answer to a request from the Anti-Slavery Bazaar in Boston in 1845. It was sent in 1847 and first published in *The Liberty Bell* (1848). (See also 'A Curse for a Nation'.) In this poem, the poet highlights the growing problem between black and white populations in America. Note how the repetition of the word 'black' enforces the message of the poem.

GLOSSARY

Pilgrim's Point place where the Pilgrim Fathers first landed

I.2 **first white pilgrims** the Pilgrim Fathers

VI.3 **cark** burden

VIII.6 **whip-poor-will; cat of the glen** corporal punishment instruments

XXXII.4 **the Washington-race** white Americans

TO FLUSH, MY DOG (PAGE 257)

The spaniel, Flush, was given to Elizabeth Barrett
Browning by her 'admired friend' Miss Mitford. The
dog became almost an obsession with the poet.

GLOSSARY

I.4 **benediction** blessing

III.3 **alchemize** alter as if by a chemical reaction

IV.2 **bland** mild / gentle

COWPER'S GRAVE (PAGE 295)

Elizabeth Barrett Browning praises Cowper's steadfast
spirit and single-minded expression of his views despite
all his worldly difficulties.

COMMENT

William Cowper (pronounced Cooper) (1731–1800)
was a poet and writer who spoke out against slavery,
amongst other things. He was a disturbed and inwardly
vexed man who dealt with what he felt was human
isolation and helplessness in this world.

GLOSSARY

VII.2 **sylvan** rural

X.4 **pathetic** sad / arousing pity

XII.2 **manifested** shown

XIV.3 **mar** spoil

CHANGE UPON CHANGE (PAGE 302)

Note how important the changing seasons are in this poem. A woman reflects bitterly that although she does not change, the man she loves does, like the seasons of the year. Apparently, women are constant, they treasure love and are happy to wait for true love. Men, however, are cruel and unpredictable and confuse passing whim for true feelings.

COMMENT   Notice how effectively the poet uses imagery (see Literary Terms) from the natural world to reflect the blossoming and death of human emotions.

GLOSSARY

l.8 mute silent

ll.10 enow enough

CATARINA TO CAMOËNS (PAGE 308)

In this poem Camoëns is portrayed as the romantic (see Literary Terms) lover of the deserted, dying Catarina, a lady of the Portuguese Court. Catarina thinks back to their happier days together.

COMMENT   Camoëns, 1542–80, was a Portuguese poet. Elizabeth Barrett Browning had read his works in translation.

This was one of Robert Browning's favourite poems and gave rise to the nickname 'Portuguese' in *Sonnets from the Portuguese.*

Notice how the refrain reinforces Catarina's pathetic situation. The poem's bitter/sweet refrain neatly mirrors Camoëns' earlier compliments to his forlorn lover. Again, the poet uses some archaic (see Literary Terms) words to create the atmosphere. Notice, too, the fluidity of the verse: lines often overrun into the next.

GLOSSARY

ll.1 burden refrain

lll.1 vesper evening

7 yestreen evening gone by

VI.5 unweeting unknowing

XII.1 **palace-lattice** palace windows

XIII.2 **gittern** a guitar-like instrument

6 **dissemble** pretend

XV.5 **Miserere** a prayer based on the Fifty-first psalm

XIX.7 **terrene** earthly, material

THE SOUL'S EXPRESSION (PAGE 328)

The poet compares her attempts to express her inner poetic feelings to that of performing music. Somehow, she feels her efforts to express her true feelings are not fully adequate.

COMMENT   This **sonnet** is an extended **metaphor** (see Literary Terms).

GLOSSARY

5 **octaves** musical sounds

8 **sensual** that which can be physically felt

14 **apocalypse of soul** true revelation of her inner feelings

PAST AND FUTURE (PAGE 329)

The poet gives thanks for what she has achieved and for what she hopes to achieve. She has recognised the value of God and of many things in life.

COMMENT   The central **image** (see Literary Terms) revolves around the idea of a wine-cup filled with potentially heady liquid.

GLOSSARY

3 **Supernal Will** according to the plans of God and Heaven

fain rather (archaic – see Literary Terms)

11 **darkling** growing dark

GRIEF (PAGE 330)

The poet states that those who feel true grief suffer in silence and do not express it in noisy lamentation.

There are those who do not realise the depth of true grief: 'Men incredulous of despair'.

COMMENT The central **metaphor** (see Literary Terms) is that true grief is like a 'monumental statue' which expresses sorrow silently. It will go on into crumbling eternity just as the really grief-stricken person will take their sorrow to the grave. 'I tell you hopeless grief is passionless': this stresses the paralysing effect of real grief.

GLOSSARY
2 **incredulous** not believing in
8 **absolute** combines the idea of absolute power and determination

THE PRISONER (PAGE 335)

Notice how glimpses of the outside world emphasise the prisoner's predicament.

Elizabeth Barrett Browning comments poignantly how a prisoner is cut off from outside life – just as she was, as an invalid in her room, 'this door so closely shut' (line 7). All 'natural' experiences become remote yet desperately valued, until they are all seen as longingly desirable, 'transfigured to Divine' (line 14).

COMMENT Note, again, how fluidly the lines run on – a style much favoured by her predecessor, John Keats.

GLOSSARY
2 **sward** lawn / grass
9 **dilated** made more indistinct
10 **fancies** imaginings
12 **precluded** numbed / unexercised

VOID IN LAW (PAGE 557)

The repetition of the word 'sleep' stresses the mother's feelings.

In this bitter lullaby the woman resents the departure of her 'husband' who has deserted her, leaving her with a new-born baby. It appears that he was legally bound to another woman before he met her. She does not accept that the man can just go off avoiding his responsibilities.

COMMENT
There is a painful tension here between the mother's enduring feelings for her lost lover and the tender love for her sleeping child. Despite all that has happened, the love of the mother and child for the man who appeared committed to them will last eternally.

GLOSSARY
III.6 **the old cards ... of yore** as in a well-known card game, the packs have been shuffled, i.e. the loved one has been tricked or jilted

XI.1 **He of the Manger** Jesus

4 **the Magi** the three kings who came to witness Christ's birth

6 **declaim** proclaim

BIANCA AMONG THE NIGHTINGALES (PAGE 560)

Bianca has been cheated in the end by an unfaithful lover despite his passionate promises and her belief in him.

COMMENT
This poem is a bitter monologue (see Literary Terms). Despite the feeling of fulfilment, it is a haunting exposure of men who woo women, make promises and then desert them (see the poem above). Men are shown as unworthy of the highest passion.

Note how the nightingale is used as a recurrent refrain (see Literary Terms). The nightingale's beautiful song has often been seen in poetry as a symbol (see Literary Terms) of passionate love, or regret or sadness (see, for example, Keats's 'Ode to a Nightingale'). The nightingales here become a cruel and menacing symbol and their song an intrusive mockery and threat to her lost love.

GLOSSARY

IV.8 **sundered** severed

VI.7 **profaned** defiled / spoiled

IX.2 **Arno's stream** the river Arno that flows through Florence

XII.5 **larcenous** thieving

XII.7 **pyx** sacred casket

XV.1 **springe** trap

THE BEST THING IN THE WORLD (PAGE 566)

This twelve-line poem expresses the poet's delight in the world about her and in the mutual satisfaction of requited love.

COMMENT   The last line: 'Something out of it, I think' has an **ironic ambiguity** (see Literary Terms) about it. The poem is a good example of Elizabeth Barrett Browning's **lyrical** (see Literary Terms) writing at its best.

GLOSSARY

2 **impearled** made like the texture of a pearl

6 **self-decked** artificially put on

8 **wink** close the eyes

A MUSICAL INSTRUMENT (PAGE 570)

Note how the rhythm and pattern echo the force of the god Pan.

This carefully fashioned and effective poem celebrates the myth of the god Pan who, it was believed, could cause frenzy ('panic') in all who heard him play upon his reed pipe. The poet imagines the god selecting and making his pipe and its after-effects.

COMMENT   The opening **stanza** sets the whole tone and **rhythmic** (see Literary Terms) pattern for the poem:

> What was he doing, the great god Pan,
> Down in the reeds by the river?
> Spreading ruin and scattering ban,
> Splashing and paddling with hooves of a goat,

And breaking the golden lilies afloat
With the dragon-fly on the river.

GLOSSARY   *I.3* **ban** harm /chaos

        II.3 **turbidly** muddily

        IV.3 **pith** the sap

THE FORCED RECRUIT – SOLFERINO, 1859 (PAGE 574)

The battle of Solferino resulted in a French and
Sardinian victory over Austrian forces in northern Italy.
The poem describes the fate of a young man of Venice
forced to fight against his will, on the Austrian side. He
was mere 'cannon-fodder' – he even had no
ammunition for his musket (rifle) – and the poet
imagines him begging for death in the Italian cause –
even if it means being killed whilst press-ganged by
Italy's enemies.

COMMENT Italy was largely under foreign domination until it
achieved unification in 1861. Living in Florence,
Elizabeth Barrett Browning was intensely interested in
Italy's fate.

GLOSSARY   *III.2* **alien the cloth on his breast** foreign badge, i.e. Austrian

        4 **blazon the brass with their names** to display names on a
        roll of honour

        X.3 **filial obedience** duty of a son (or daughter) to their
        parents or a national cause

Identify to whom or to what these lines refer.

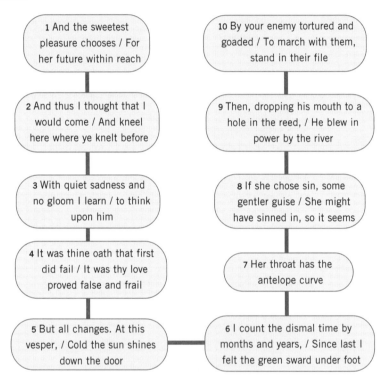

1 And the sweetest pleasure chooses / For her future within reach

10 By your enemy tortured and goaded / To march with them, stand in their file

2 And thus I thought that I would come / And kneel here where ye knelt before

9 Then, dropping his mouth to a hole in the reed, / He blew in power by the river

3 With quiet sadness and no gloom I learn / to think upon him

8 If she chose sin, some gentler guise / She might have sinned in, so it seems

4 It was thine oath that first did fail / It was thy love proved false and frail

7 Her throat has the antelope curve

5 But all changes. At this vesper, / Cold the sun shines down the door

6 I count the dismal time by months and years, / Since last I felt the green sward under foot

Check your answers on page 56.

Consider these issues.

a Examine the theme of the cruelty of fate as seen in 'The Romance of the Swan's Nest'.

b Look at the ways in which 'The Runaway Slave at Pilgrim's Point' deals with the problems of racial abuse.

c Examine the themes of desertion and regret in 'Catarina to Camoëns' and 'Bianca Among the Nightingales'.

d Consider how Elizabeth Barrett Browning deals with the misfortunes of war in 'The Forced Recruit'.

Section 3: The Longer Poems

Casa Guidi Windows (page 340)

Both parts of this highly original poem appeared in May 1851. 'Casa Guidi' was the Browning's home in Florence. Elizabeth Barrett Browning's poem is a brilliant eye-witness account of what she had heard and understood about what was happening in the political atmosphere around her. It is a 'journalistic diary' of the Italian struggle for independence against Austria and the movement towards Italian unification. The poem has a commitment and strength of style which are typified in the two extracts which follow.

Comment   The poetic form in which she writes is an achievement in itself. She sustains the **rhythm** and flow of the lines using a basic ten-syllable line – the **pentameter** and repeated **rhymes**. The effect of the movement of the lines, especially, again, when read aloud, is both **colloquial** (see Literary Terms) and emotional. The second extract recreates the excitement of the moment in all its fervour and feeling.

Part I
lines 1–19
(pages 340–1)

I HEARD last night a little child go singing
'Neath Casa Guidi windows, by the church,
O bella libertà, O bella! stringing
The same words still on notes he went in search
So high for, you concluded the upspringing
Of such a nimble bird to sky from perch
Must leave the whole in a tremble green,
And that the heart of Italy must beat,
While such a voice had leave to rise serene
'Twixt church and palace of a Florence street!
A little child, too, who not long had been
By mother's finger steadied on his feet.
And still *O bella libertà* he sang.

Then I thought, musing, of the innumerous
Sweet songs which still for Italy outrang
From older singers' lips, who sang not thus

Exultingly and purely, yet with pang
Fast sheathed in music, touched the heart of us
So finely, that the pity scarcely pained.

Part II
lines 118–29
(page 362)

Consider how the
poet's language
indicates the
feeling of
excitement here.

Long live the people! How they lived! and boiled
And bubbled in the cauldron of the street.
How the young blustered nor the old recoiled, –
And what a thunderous stir of tongues and feet
Trod flat the palpitating bells, and foiled
The joy-guns of their echo, shattering it!
How down they pulled the Duke's arms everywhere!
How up they set new café-signs, to show
Where patriots might sip ices in pure air –
(The fresh paint smelling somewhat).
To and fro
How marched the civic guard, and stopped to stare
When boys broke windows in a civic glow.
How rebel songs were sung to loyal tunes,
And bishops cursed the ecclesiastic metres.

GLOSSARY

1.3 **'O bella libertà, O bella!'** Oh how beautiful is liberty, Oh how beautiful

5 **upspringing** a poetic coinage (see Versification, Language & Imagery) for suddenly rising into flight

10 **'Twixt church and palace** taken literally it means physically between the church and the palace. In another sense, it could mean the political struggle between the church authorities and the ruling classes

12 **By mother's fingers steadied on his feet** a very touching image of the mother helping the child to take its first faltering steps. Perhaps this parallels the Italian people's first faltering steps towards independence and reunification

15 **outrang** another poetic coinage (see Versification, Language & Imagery) meaning sang out / performed in song

AURORA LEIGH (PAGE 374)

This was Elizabeth Barrett Browning's longest and most ambitious poem and was published in 1856. In it,

This poem is now becoming a focus of increasing interest for feminists (see Literary Terms) and literary commentaries. she generally champions the right of women to intellectual freedom and is concerned with the position of the female artist in society. She described it as 'A Novel in Verse'. It is the life-story of a woman writer. In the poem, she is also concerned with the 'poet's mission' and sums up what she sees as the poet's purpose in influencing society.

COMMENT   There are some excellent observations of social groups and attitudes as well as descriptions of the English countryside and Italian landscapes.

POEMS BEFORE CONGRESS

All the poems in this volume of poetry (published in 1860) reflect the poet's concern with Italy's fate.

AN AUGUST VOICE (PAGE 549)

The poet imagines the lines are spoken by Napoleon III of France who had sided his country with Italy hoping to expel the Austrians from Italy when the Second War of Independence broke out in 1859.

GLOSSARY

I.4 **Dall Ongaro** Francesco Dall'Ongaro, a popular poet and supporter of liberty

5 **Ricasoli** Baron Bettino Ricasoli, a leader of the moderates

III.4 **Forty-eight** an ironic (see Literary Terms) reference to the uprisings of 1848

8 **Proprio motu** spontaneously

IV.4 **Radetsky** Marshal Joseph Radetsky (1766–1858) had been a forceful commander of Austrian forces in Italy

VII.2 **Pitti** Palazzo Pitti, a palatial royal residence in Florence

XI.7 **Poniatowsky** Jozef Poniatowsky (1816–73), originally a member of the Tuscan parliament

A CURSE FOR A NATION (PAGE 554)

See how the form of this poem and its language emphasise the poet's indignation.

At the time of its publication this poem was wrongly interpreted as an attack on Britain because of its attitude to Napoleon III and Italian nationalism. In fact the poem was written at the request of the Anti-Slavery Bazaar in Boston. (See Section 2, 'A Runaway Slave at Pilgrim's Point'.) The American slave laws is its main theme, therefore.

COMMENT

It reads as an excellent and forceful poem, especially when read aloud. It is interesting to do this with two speakers, one reading the 'Prologue' and one 'The Curse'. The poem, with its carefully constructed pattern, thunders with indignation.

GLOSSARY

Prologue

The Curse

4 **Western Sea** the Atlantic Ocean

29 **oligarchic** ruled by a select few

I.9 **acolyte** an assistant / a novice

II.16 **feudal law** a law requiring inferiors to show unswerving allegiance to their superiors

Identify to whom or to what these lines refer.

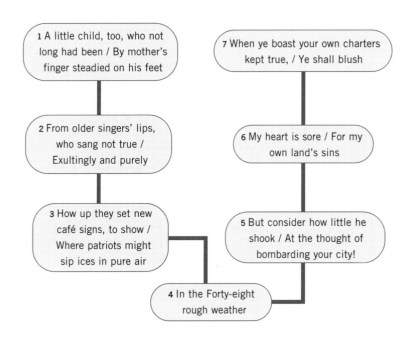

1 A little child, too, who not long had been / By mother's finger steadied on his feet

7 When ye boast your own charters kept true, / Ye shall blush

2 From older singers' lips, who sang not true / Exultingly and purely

6 My heart is sore / For my own land's sins

3 How up they set new café signs, to show / Where patriots might sip ices in pure air

5 But consider how little he shook / At the thought of bombarding your city!

4 In the Forty-eight rough weather

Check your answers on page 56.

Consider these issues.

a In the extracts from *Casa Guidi Windows*, consider how Elizabeth Barrett Browning shows a refreshingly 'modern' use of language and ideas.

b Notice how the constant use of repetition adds to the force of 'An August Voice' and 'A curse for a Nation'.

c Consider ways in which the poet shows her skill in narrative writing.

d List the ways the poems in this section can be considered to be **didactic** (see Literary Terms).

PART THREE

COMMENTARY

THEMES

CLASSICAL GREECE AND ROME

The classics were a lifelong absorption.

From her earliest years, Elizabeth Barrett Browning showed a lively interest in self-education and learning. When very young she had taught herself Ancient Greek and had read widely in the classical authors, European and English literature and contemporary serious periodicals. The classics were one of the greatest influences as she developed as a poet towards her ambition – to be accepted as a committed and respected writer. We see classical influence early in her life in such poems as 'The Battle of Marathon' written at the age of eight, and her translation of 'Prometheus Bound', the latter from the Greek of Aeschylus. Later she would continue to display her passionate interest in Greek subject matter in such a poem as 'A Musical Instrument' which celebrates the myth of the god Pan.

POLITICAL AND SOCIAL ISSUES

Elizabeth was very socially aware and had an informed outlook.

At a time when women were still not expected to be widely educated, she vied with her brothers, especially her favourite 'Bro', to be on as equal a footing as was possible and acceptable. It also helped to counterbalance the stultifying situation at home where her father ruled without question. She showed concern for current political and social issues at home and abroad. This can be seen in such a poem as 'The Cry of the Children' which is an impassioned plea for reform of the factory conditions of the time. The problems of racial intolerance and slavery were met head on in 'The Runaway Slave at Pilgrim's Point' and the later

'A Curse for a Nation' highlights the increasing racial
tensions between blacks and whites in America.

LOVE AND WOMEN'S ROLE IN SOCIETY

*Elizabeth
questioned the
relationship
between the sexes.*

'Catarina to Camoëns' and 'Bianca Among the
Nightingales' both show influences of European
literature as well as the theme of a woman loved and
wronged looking back over time and lamenting men's
fickleness. This element is revealed in several other
poems for example: 'Proof and Disproof' and 'Void in
Law'. Women are frequently seen as victims and men as
faithless and disloyal. She always continued to display
an incisive view of the relationship between man and
woman. Yet a sense of nostalgia remained in many of
her poems, for example, in 'The Prisoner'.

Her love for Robert Browning and their secret marriage
and elopement to the continent transformed her life.
Her *Sonnets from the Portuguese* show a touching and
searching development of her feelings of love and, along
with her lyric (see Literary Terms) poems are
considered amongst her greatest achievements. The
couple's mutual happiness in their married life and her
apparently remarkable recovery from earlier illness
imbued her poems with a renewed vigour. However,
family life and the role of women in society remained
an abiding interest.

Her long narrative 'novel-poem' *Aurora Leigh* grapples
with the theme of the woman writer in society and
how to resolve that position in a somewhat hostile
world.

ITALIAN UNIFICATION

A greater political and social concern is shown in 'The
Forced Recruit'. With *Casa Guidi Windows* she reveals

an almost 'modern' tone in theme and language. *Poems Before Congress* continue the themes of the rights and wrongs of the European people's struggle against autocracy but references to social problems at home recur as, for example, in 'A Curse for a Nation' where she again alludes to the sufferings of the underprivileged:

> My heart is sore
> For my own land's sins: for little feet
> Of children bleeding along the street.

For a woman in the early nineteenth century Elizabeth was advanced in her political views.   As a poet, Elizabeth Barrett Browning was, at the time of her marriage, widely respected and better known for her writing than her husband, Robert. Long after her death, Robert Browning wrote the following tribute to his wife: 'The simple truth is that *she* was the poet, and I the clever person by comparison.'

VERSIFICATION, LANGUAGE & IMAGERY

Elizabeth Barrett Browning's poetry may be divided into at least four types of verse.

THE BALLAD OR ROMANCE

As in such a poem as 'The Romance of the Swan's Nest' there is no particular pattern to the **ballad** (see Literary Terms) except that it usually contains:
- a refrain at the end of each **stanza** (see Literary Terms), sometimes altered each time to take the story further on
- a highly structured **rhyme** scheme to make it memorable
- an element of the strange or the fanciful or the exaggerated

THE LYRIC

In such poems as 'A Seaside Walk' or 'Proof and Disproof' there is no particular pattern. However, lyrical (see Literary Terms) poetry is characterised by:

- a song-like structured rhyme scheme
- an easily remembered rhythm
- subject matter that concerns itself with the poet's deep emotions

THE NARRATIVE

In such a poem as *Casa Guidi Windows* the poet is using mainly iambic pentameters (see Literary Terms) to tell a story. Obviously other forms of poetry tell some story but the distinguishing feature of the narrative poem is usually its pattern and length.

THE SONNET

Such poems have characteristically a fourteen-line structure. Added to this they have a strict rhyme scheme and use basically iambic pentameters (see Literary Terms). The rhyme scheme used by Elizabeth Barrett Browning is basically: abba abba cdcdcd.

- The sonnet (see Literary Terms) form is well suited to the expression of a poet's feelings and emotions and usually concerns one central idea.

Her sonnets were   • A sonnet sequence (see Literary Terms) is a group of
amongst her most   sonnets written on one developing subject such as
popular writings.   *Sonnets from the Portuguese* which concerns itself with the progress of the love between the poet and Robert Browning.

ARCHAISMS AND ARCHAIC LANGUAGE

In many of her poems, Elizabeth Barrett Browning uses archaisms / archaic language (see Literary Terms).

These are often introduced to create an 'authentic' tone of older poetry as for example the use of 'steed', 'nathelees', 'gage', 'guerdon', 'troth', 'ye' in 'The Romance of the Swan's Nest' or 'yestereen' and 'unweeting' in 'Catarina to Camoëns'. This use of language can be somewhat irritating to the contemporary reader but it is worth considering it in its context and recognising that the choice of such vocabulary by the poet was for considered reasons.

COINAGES OF WORDS

As with many poets, Elizabeth Barrett Browning could be adept at adapting vocabulary to bring out a forceful word or expression. We can see this in such words as 'impearled' in 'The Best Thing in the World' and 'upspringing' and 'outrang' in the extracts from *Casa Guidi Windows*.

IMAGERY

Study her grasp of imagery and observation.

There are many moments in Elizabeth Barrett Browning's poetry when she hits just the right choice of words and image (see Literary Terms) to sparkle with effective meaning. This is the achievement of true poetic awareness. The following are a few examples:

And tulips, children love to stretch
Their fingers down. ('A Flower in a Letter')

The bee that once did suck thee,
And build thy perfumed ambers up his hive. ('A Dead Rose')

March winds violate my springs ('Proof and Disproof')

Nuts lie in thy path for stones,
And thy feast-day macaroons
Turn to daily rations! ('To Flush, My Dog')

Like saturated sponges ('Bianca Among the Nightingales')

Her throat has the antelope curve ('Void in Law')

INNOVATIVE RHYMING

Elizabeth Barrett Browning took an especial interest in the effect of rhyme and prided herself on being congratulated on her novelty and innovation. She was sometimes considered to be too ingenious with her use of half-rhymes (see Literary Terms), and assonance (see Literary Terms). Yet she valued such technical devices in her poetry. A few examples will suffice:

- gathered / withered ('A Dead Rose')
- father / gather (' The Cry of the Children')
- mouth / truth ('My Kate')
- yes / answerless ('Proof and Disproof')

Above all she was a consummate 'arranger of words, phrases and rhythms' and excelled in the lilting and haunting melodies of lyrical (see Literary Terms) and mournful Romance (see Literary Terms). It is for this type of poetry that she is especially remembered and enjoyed.

PART FOUR

STUDY SKILLS

HOW TO USE QUOTATIONS

One of the secrets of success in writing essays is the way you use quotations. There are five basic principles:

- Put inverted commas at the beginning and end of the quotation
- Write the quotation exactly as it appears in the original
- Do not use a quotation that repeats what you have just written
- Use the quotation so that it fits into your sentence
- Keep the quotation as short as possible

Quotations should be used to develop the line of thought in your essays.

Your comment should not duplicate what is in your quotation. For example:

> We can see in 'A Dead Rose' how the poet is able to describe well the minuteness of a fly's feet by comparing them to tendrils: 'The fly that 'lit upon thee / To stretch the tendrils of its tiny feet.'

Far more effective is to write:

> We see 'In A Dead Rose' how the poet creates a strikingly apt metaphor: 'The fly that 'lit upon thee / To stretch the tendrils of its tiny feet.'

Always lay out the lines as they appear in the text. For example:

> The poet writes a strikingly apt metaphor when she writes:
> 'The fly that 'lit upon thee
> To stretch the tendrils of its tiny feet.'

or:

> The poet writes a strikingly apt metaphor when she writes: 'The fly that 'lit upon thee / To stretch the tendrils of its tiny feet.'

However, the most sophisticated way of using the writer's words is to embed them into your sentence:

The use of the expression 'the tendrils of its tiny feet' illustrates the poet's ability to select a strikingly apt metaphor.

When you use quotations in this way, you are demonstrating the ability to use text as evidence to support your ideas.

Essay writing

Everyone writes differently. Work through the suggestions given here and adapt the advice to suit your own style and interests. This will improve your essay-writing skills and allow your personal voice to emerge.

The following points indicate in ascending order the skills of essay writing:

- Picking out one or two facts about the story and adding the odd detail
- Writing about the text by retelling the story
- Retelling the story and adding a quotation here and there
- Organising an answer which explains what is happening in the text and giving quotations to support what you write

....

- Writing in such a way as to show that you have thought about the intentions of the writer of the text and that you understand the techniques used
- Writing at some length, giving your viewpoint on the text and commenting by picking out details to support your views
- Looking at the text as a work of art, demonstrating clear critical judgement and explaining to the reader of your essay how the enjoyment of the text is

assisted by literary devices, linguistic effects and psychological insights; showing how the text relates to the time when it was written

The dotted line above represents the division between lower- and higher-level grades. Higher-level performance begins when you start to consider your response as a reader of the text. The highest level is reached when you offer an enthusiastic personal response and show how this piece of literature is a product of its time.

Coursework essay

Set aside an hour or so at the start of your work to plan what you have to do.

- List all the points you feel are needed to cover the task. Collect page references of information and quotations that will support what you have to say. A helpful tool is the highlighter pen: this saves painstaking copying and enables you to target precisely what you want to use.

- Focus on what you consider to be the main points of the essay. Try to sum up your argument in a single sentence, which could be the closing sentence of your essay. Depending on the essay title, it could be a statement of the subject of the poem: In 'The Prisoner' Elizabeth Barrett Browning shows how isolation from the outside world makes that very world all the more precious; an opinion about setting: In 'Bianca Among the Nightingales' the bitter sadness of the situation is emphasised by the constant references to the birds' overpowering and almost menacing song; or a summary of the underlying theme: The main theme of a poem such as 'Void in Law' is the desertion of the woman and the faithlessness of men.

- Make a short essay plan. Use the first paragraph to introduce the argument you wish to make. In the following paragraphs develop this argument with details, examples and other possible points of view.

Sum up your argument in the last paragraph. Check you have answered the question.

- Write the essay, remembering all the time the central point you are making.
- On completion, go back over what you have written to eliminate careless errors and improve expression. Read it aloud to yourself, or, if you are feeling more confident, to a relative or friend.

If you can, try to type your essay, using a word processor. This will allow you to correct and improve your writing without spoiling its appearance.

Examination essay

The essay written in an examination often carries more marks than the coursework essay even though it is written under considerable time pressure.

In the revision period build up notes on various aspects of the text you are using. Fortunately, in acquiring this set of York Notes on *Elizabeth Barrett Browning: Selected Poems*, you have made a prudent beginning! York Notes are set out to give you vital information and help you to construct your personal overview of the text.

Make notes with appropriate quotations about the key issues of the set text. Go into the examination knowing your text and having a clear set of opinions about it.

In most English Literature examinations you can take in copies of your set books. This in an enormous advantage although it may lull you into a false sense of security. Beware! There is simply not enough time in an examination to read the book from scratch.

In the examination

- Read the question paper carefully and remind yourself what you have to do.
- Look at the questions on your set texts to select the one that most interests you and mentally work out the points you wish to stress.
- Remind yourself of the time available and how you are going to use it.

- Briefly map out a short plan in note form that will keep your writing on track and illustrate the key argument you want to make.
- Then set about writing it.
- When you have finished, check through to eliminate errors.

To summarise, these are the keys to success:

- **Know the text**
- **Have a clear understanding of and opinions on the storyline, characters, setting, themes and writer's concerns**
- **Select the right material**
- **Plan and write a clear response, continually bearing the question in mind**

SAMPLE ESSAY PLAN

A typical essay question on the poetry of Elizabeth Barrett Browning is followed by a sample essay plan in note form. This does not present the only answer to the question, merely one. Always try to use your own ideas.

Write about two of Elizabeth Barrett Browning's poems which have had a strong effect upon you.

Part 1
Introduction

The two poems selected: 'The Cry of the Children' and 'A Dead Rose'.

Each poem is concerned with two of the main issues which concerned Elizabeth Barrett Browning. 'The Cry of the Children' with social / political issues, 'A Dead Rose' with the concept of regret and an awareness of the sadness at the passing of time.

Part 2
'The Cry of the Children'

Some comment on the position of children working in factories and their suffering. The pattern and rhyme effectively emphasise the feeling of pity for the children and the helplessness of those adults who are aware of this. We are moved to feel we all have some responsibility for all this. This causes us to consider similar issues rife today.

Part 3
'A Dead Rose'

A good example of Elizabeth Barrett Browning's lyrical poetry. Carefully fashioned with a strict rhyme scheme however, this patterning does not intrude. Language and meaning skilfully, yet poignantly, handled. The rose is a symbol acting as a trigger to associated memories.

Part 4
Conclusion

Some comment on unusual or interesting language and how it influences the reader's view. Final re-emphasis of the effect of the poems.

Make a plan as previously shown and attempt these questions.

1 Choose two poems which tell a story. Suggest how the poet makes these poems interesting.

2 Choose two poems which express ideas or emotions powerfully. Explain how ideas or emotions are expressed in each poem.

3 Write about three poems which show how love, in a variety of situations, is presented by Elizabeth Barrett Browning.

4 Choose any three poems which have made you interested in the poet's language as well as in what the poet has to say.

5 Write about three poems which interested you because of the unusual treatment of love and emotion.

6 How are different aspects of love shown in three or four of Elizabeth Barrett Browning's poems?

7 Write about the ways in which Elizabeth Barrett Browning conveys strong feelings in her poetry. You should refer to at least three poems.

8 Love poems can be written in many different ways and for a variety of purposes. Write about three or four of Elizabeth Barrett Browning's poems which show this variety. Explain how the way they are written reflects their content and purpose.

CULTURAL CONNECTIONS

BROADER PERSPECTIVES

There is no doubt that Elizabeth Barrett Browning's poetry has been underestimated since her time as to its value and influence. After her death she appeared to be overshadowed by such major figures of Victorian literature as Tennyson, and her husband Robert Browning. Yet, we should remember that Robert Browning himself expressed his regard for her works as well as his love for her as a woman. It is being increasingly realised that her **feminist** (see Literary Terms) voice dealt with issues ahead of her time as did her concern for social and political inequalities. Elizabeth Barrett Browning, as we have seen, concerned herself with many social and political issues, freedoms which perhaps today we take for granted. Far from the usual picture of a weary and sickly **romantic** (see Literary Terms) writer of verse, Elizabeth Barrett Browning wrote intensely political poems ('The Runaway Slave at Pilgrim's Point' and 'A Curse for a Nation' amongst others).

There is no doubt that had she lived longer, her sympathies toward social and political reform would have found true recognition. It was for literary figures such as Dickens and Elizabeth Gaskell to highlight the hardships of the poor and underprivileged in the later part of the nineteenth century.

Elizabeth Barrett Browning's feminist enlightenment is being increasingly recognised in the late twentieth century.

FURTHER READING

Try reading some of the Romantic (see Context &
Setting) poets who preceded Elizabeth Barrett
Browning and see if you can notice similarities and
influences. Read: John Keats's 'The Eve of St Agnes',
'La Belle Dame sans Merci' and 'Ode to Autumn';
Percy Bysshe Shelley's 'Ode to Liberty' and 'Ode to
Naples'; Wordsworth's 'Lucy', 'The Solitary Reaper',
'Perfect Woman' and 'The Rainbow'.

Look at earlier writers like William Blake who wrote
simple, powerful poems about the plight of the
underprivileged, for example: 'The Little Black Boy',
'The Chimney Sweeper' and 'On Anothers Sorrow'.

Read Harriet Beecher Stowe's exciting early novel about
slavery: *Uncle Tom's Cabin* (1852), which stirred up
great public feeling at the time of its publication. You
will also find parallel concerns in Charles Dickens's
novels: *Hard Times* (1854), for example, is very critical
of working conditions in factories and the workers'
desperate slum life, centred round one of his characters
called Stephen Blackpool; Elizabeth Gaskell has similar
concerns in *Mary Barton* (1848); Henry Mayhew's
London Labour and the London Poor (1851) is a very
readable and interesting investigation into the seemy
low life of the very poor in Victorian London.
Although not published until after Elizabeth Barrett
Browning's death, Charles Kingsley's *Water Babies*
(1863) about the plight of child chimney sweeps, shows
in its subject matter parallel concerns to Elizabeth
Barrett Browning's work.

Look in an encyclopedia to find out about radical social
reformers who influenced Elizabeth Barrett Browning:
Thomas Paine (1737–1809) whose most famous work
was *The Rights of Man*; the French writer Voltaire
(1694–1778), whose witty *Candide* exposed many of the

evils of his times; Mary Wollstonecraft (1759–97) whose *A Vindication of the Rights of Woman* could be claimed to be the book which inspired the modern feminist movement; and William Wilberforce (1759–1833) who worked to suppress slavery in the British Empire.

A study of the poems mentioned in these Notes will give you an adequate working knowledge of the poetry of Elizabeth Barrett Browning. However, if you want to explore her life and work further, the following books might be of interest:

Peter Dally, *Elizabeth Barrett Browning: A Psychological Portrait* (Macmillan, London, 1989)

Margaret Forster, *Elizabeth Barrett Browning, A biography* (Chatto & Windus, London, 1988)

Colin Graham, ed., *Elizabeth Barrett Browning* (Everyman's Poetry, J.M. Dent, London, 1998)

Alethea Haytor, *Mrs Browning: A Poet's Work and its Setting* (Faber & Faber, London, 1962)

Dorothy Hewlett, *Elizabeth Barrett Browning: A Life* (Cassell, London, 1953)

Malcolm Hicks, ed., *Elizabeth Barrett Browning, selected poems* (Carcanet, 1988)

Cora Kaplan, *Aurora Leigh and Other Poems* (The Women's Press, London, 1978)

Angela Leighton, *Elizabeth Barrett Browning* (Harvester Press, Brighton, 1986)

Gardner B. Taplin, *The Life of Elizabeth Barrett Browning* (John Murray, London, 1957)

ambiguous / ambiguity the capacity for words and sentences to have more than one meaning

apostrophe a rhetorical term for a speech addressed to a person, idea or thing

archaisms / archaic language the use of out of date words or expressions for a particular effect

assonance repetition, in a sequence of words, of the same vowel with differing consonants between, e.g. 'child' and 'silence'

ballad a poem which tells a story in a colloquial / familiar way

bathos an anti-climax

colloquial the use of language of everyday speech as opposed to formal language or 'poetic' language

didactic / didacticism literature that is designed to instruct or educate

elegiac concerned with lamentation and death

epitaph an inscription on a tomb, or a piece of writing suitable for it

feminism a passionate belief in the value of women's intellect and emotions and their right to equality with men

foot section of a line of verse

iambic / iambic pentameter referring to a foot of verse consisting of a weak stressed syllable followed by a strongly stressed one; a pentameter contains basically five feet, making ten syllables in all

imagery / image language in which metaphors and similes are used. More generally, the word is used to cover all words appealing to the senses or feelings

irony / ironic words or expressions which are capable of secondary meaning sometimes causing hidden amusement; sometimes achieved through understatement: 'The Forty-eight rough weather'

lyric / lyrical usually a short song-like poem that expresses a personal, intense emotion

melodramatic writing tending towards the sensational or exaggerated

metaphor figure of speech in which something is compared to something which it resembles, without using 'like' or 'as'

metre regulated succession of groups of syllables creating a pattern. It is based on the use of long and short or stressed and unstressed syllables

monologue a single person speaking with or without an audience

narrative a telling of a story or a recital of facts

pathos, pathetic evoking strong feelings of pity

pentameter see iambic pentameter

personification a variety of figurative or metaphorical language in which things or ideas are treated as if they were human beings, with human attributes and feelings

poetic diction the particular choice of vocabulary used by the poet

poetic pose / voice an attitude by which a writer takes on a position removed from the subject of their writing even though they are expressing their own involvement

refrain words or lines that are repeated in the course of a poem

rhetoric especially in a speech, designed to persuade. In Elizabeth Barrett Browning's poetry, she attempts to do this especially in such poems as 'Poems Before Congress'

rhyme often referred to as 'chiming' – usually on the last syllable of a line. Such effects aim at a melodious resonance at the end of such lines. half-rhyme imperfect rhymes that look apparently right because of their spelling, but which are pronounced differently. Sometimes referred to as eye-rhymes

rhythm variation on the level of emphasis placed on syllables

Romance originally writings that concerned themselves with heroic deeds, knightly quests, magic, the supernatural and love. These often had a moral framework

romance / romantic connected with love, imagination and the fanciful

simile poetic image which compares two things by indicating the similarities between them. It usually contains the words 'like' or 'as'

sonnet / sonnet sequence a poem of iambic pentameter, written in fourteen lines and with a strict rhyme pattern (see Language & Imagery)

stanza a verse, a unit of several lines of verse

symbol / symbolise some word or idea that represents something else by association or emotional memory

TEST ANSWERS

TEST YOURSELF (Section 1)

 1 The suffering children, 'The Cry of the Children'
2 A withered flower, 'A Flower in a Letter'
3 The dead rose, 'A Dead Rose'
4 Sleep given by God, 'The Sleep'
5 Her loved-one's inner thoughts, 'Proof and Disproof'
6 The poet's letters, *Sonnets from the Portuguese*, XXVIII
7 A kiss, *Sonnets from the Portuguese*, XXXVIII
8 Kate, 'My Kate'
9 The poet and her feelings, 'My Heart and I'

TEST YOURSELF (Section 2)

 1 Little Ellie, 'Romance of the Swan's Nest'
2 The black fugitive appealing to the spirits of the Pilgrim Fathers, 'The Runaway Slave at Pilgrim's Point'
3 William Cowper, 'Cowper's Grave'
4 The forsaken loved-one, 'Change upon Change'
5 Catarina on her death-bed, 'Catarina to Camoëns'

6 The poet confined to her room, 'The Prisoner'
7 The baby of the abandoned mother, 'Void in Law'
8 The woman whom Bianca's lover deserted her for, 'Bianca Among the Nightingales'
9 The god Pan playing his pipe, 'A Musical Instrument'
10 The Italian forced to fight for the Austrians, 'The Forced Recruit – Solferino 1859'

TEST YOURSELF (Section 3)

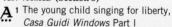 1 The young child singing for liberty, *Casa Guidi Windows* Part I
2 'Sweet songs', *Casa Guidi Windows* Part I
3 The people, *Casa Guidi Windows* Part II
4 The 1848 uprisings in Europe, 'An August Voice'
5 The Grand Duke, 'An August Voice'
6 The poet referring to England, 'A Curse for a Nation' Prologue
7 The American People / government, 'A Curse for a Nation' The Curse

Notes

NOTES

York Notes Advanced (£3.99 each)

Margaret Atwood
The Handmaid's Tale

Jane Austen
Mansfield Park

Jane Austen
Persuasion

Jane Austen
Pride and Prejudice

Alan Bennett
Talking Heads

William Blake
Songs of Innocence and of Experience

Charlotte Brontë
Jane Eyre

Emily Brontë
Wuthering Heights

Geoffrey Chaucer
The Franklin's Tale

Geoffrey Chaucer
General Prologue to the Canterbury Tales

Geoffrey Chaucer
The Wife of Bath's Prologue and Tale

Joseph Conrad
Heart of Darkness

Charles Dickens
Great Expectations

John Donne
Selected Poems

George Eliot
The Mill on the Floss

F. Scott Fitzgerald
The Great Gatsby

E.M. Forster
A Passage to India

Brian Friel
Translations

Thomas Hardy
The Mayor of Casterbridge

Thomas Hardy
Tess of the d'Urbervilles

Seamus Heaney
Selected Poems from Opened Ground

Nathaniel Hawthorne
The Scarlet Letter

James Joyce
Dubliners

John Keats
Selected Poems

Christopher Marlowe
Doctor Faustus

Arthur Miller
Death of a Salesman

Toni Morrison
Beloved

William Shakespeare
Antony and Cleopatra

William Shakespeare
As You Like It

William Shakespeare
Hamlet

William Shakespeare
King Lear

William Shakespeare
Measure for Measure

William Shakespeare
The Merchant of Venice

William Shakespeare
Much Ado About Nothing

William Shakespeare
Othello

William Shakespeare
Romeo and Juliet

William Shakespeare
The Tempest

William Shakespeare
The Winter's Tale

Mary Shelley
Frankenstein

Alice Walker
The Color Purple

Oscar Wilde
The Importance of Being Earnest

Tennessee Williams
A Streetcar Named Desire

John Webster
The Duchess of Malfi

W.B. Yeats
Selected Poems

OTHER TITLES

GCSE and equivalent levels (£3.50 each)

Maya Angelou
I Know Why the Caged Bird Sings

Jane Austen
Pride and Prejudice

Alan Ayckbourn
Absent Friends

Elizabeth Barrett Browning
Selected Poems

Robert Bolt
A Man for All Seasons

Harold Brighouse
Hobson's Choice

Charlotte Brontë
Jane Eyre

Emily Brontë
Wuthering Heights

Shelagh Delaney
A Taste of Honey

Charles Dickens
David Copperfield

Charles Dickens
Great Expectations

Charles Dickens
Hard Times

Charles Dickens
Oliver Twist

Roddy Doyle
Paddy Clarke Ha Ha Ha

George Eliot
Silas Marner

George Eliot
The Mill on the Floss

William Golding
Lord of the Flies

Oliver Goldsmith
She Stoops To Conquer

Willis Hall
The Long and the Short and the Tall

Thomas Hardy
Far from the Madding Crowd

Thomas Hardy
The Mayor of Casterbridge

Thomas Hardy
Tess of the d'Urbervilles

Thomas Hardy
The Withered Arm and other Wessex Tales

L.P. Hartley
The Go-Between

Seamus Heaney
Selected Poems

Susan Hill
I'm the King of the Castle

Barry Hines
A Kestrel for a Knave

Louise Lawrence
Children of the Dust

Harper Lee
To Kill a Mockingbird

Laurie Lee
Cider with Rosie

Arthur Miller
The Crucible

Arthur Miller
A View from the Bridge

Robert O'Brien
Z for Zachariah

Frank O'Connor
My Oedipus Complex and other stories

George Orwell
Animal Farm

J.B. Priestley
An Inspector Calls

Willy Russell
Educating Rita

Willy Russell
Our Day Out

J.D. Salinger
The Catcher in the Rye

William Shakespeare
Henry IV Part 1

William Shakespeare
Henry V

William Shakespeare
Julius Caesar

William Shakespeare
Macbeth

William Shakespeare
The Merchant of Venice

William Shakespeare
A Midsummer Night's Dream

William Shakespeare
Much Ado About Nothing

William Shakespeare
Romeo and Juliet

William Shakespeare
The Tempest

William Shakespeare
Twelfth Night

George Bernard Shaw
Pygmalion

Mary Shelley
Frankenstein

R.C. Sherriff
Journey's End

Rukshana Smith
Salt on the snow

John Steinbeck
Of Mice and Men

Robert Louis Stevenson
Dr Jekyll and Mr Hyde

Jonathan Swift
Gulliver's Travels

Robert Swindells
Daz 4 Zoe

Mildred D. Taylor
Roll of Thunder, Hear My Cry

Mark Twain
Huckleberry Finn

James Watson
Talking in Whispers

William Wordsworth
Selected Poems

A Choice of Poets

Mystery Stories of the Nineteenth Century including The Signalman

Nineteenth Century Short Stories

Poetry of the First World War

Six Women Poets

Chinua Achebe
Things Fall Apart

Edward Albee
Who's Afraid of Virginia Woolf?

Margaret Atwood
Cat's Eye

Jane Austen
Emma

Jane Austen
Northanger Abbey

Jane Austen
Sense and Sensibility

Samuel Beckett
Waiting for Godot

Robert Browning
Selected Poems

Robert Burns
Selected Poems

Angela Carter
Nights at the Circus

Geoffrey Chaucer
The Merchant's Tale

Geoffrey Chaucer
The Miller's Tale

Geoffrey Chaucer
The Nun's Priest's Tale

Samuel Taylor Coleridge
Selected Poems

Daniel Defoe
Moll Flanders

Daniel Defoe
Robinson Crusoe

Charles Dickens
Bleak House

Charles Dickens
Hard Times

Emily Dickinson
Selected Poems

Carol Ann Duffy
Selected Poems

George Eliot
Middlemarch

T.S. Eliot
The Waste Land

T.S. Eliot
Selected Poems

Henry Fielding
Joseph Andrews

E.M. Forster
Howards End

John Fowles
The French Lieutenant's Woman

Robert Frost
Selected Poems

Elizabeth Gaskell
North and South

Stella Gibbons
Cold Comfort Farm

Graham Greene
Brighton Rock

Thomas Hardy
Jude the Obscure

Thomas Hardy
Selected Poems

Joseph Heller
Catch-22

Homer
The Iliad

Homer
The Odyssey

Gerard Manley Hopkins
Selected Poems

Aldous Huxley
Brave New World

Kazuo Ishiguro
The Remains of the Day

Ben Jonson
The Alchemist

Ben Jonson
Volpone

James Joyce
A Portrait of the Artist as a Young Man

Philip Larkin
Selected Poems

D.H. Lawrence
The Rainbow

D.H. Lawrence
Selected Stories

D.H. Lawrence
Sons and Lovers

D.H. Lawrence
Women in Love

John Milton
Paradise Lost Bks I & II

John Milton
Paradise Lost Bks IV & IX

Thomas More
Utopia

Sean O'Casey
Juno and the Paycock

George Orwell
Nineteen Eighty-four

John Osborne
Look Back in Anger

Wilfred Owen
Selected Poems

Sylvia Plath
Selected Poems

Alexander Pope
Rape of the Lock and other poems

Ruth Prawer Jhabvala
Heat and Dust

Jean Rhys
Wide Sargasso Sea

William Shakespeare
As You Like It

William Shakespeare
Coriolanus

William Shakespeare
Henry IV Pt 1

William Shakespeare
Henry V

William Shakespeare
Julius Caesar

William Shakespeare
Macbeth

William Shakespeare
Measure for Measure

William Shakespeare
A Midsummer Night's Dream

William Shakespeare
Richard II

William Shakespeare
Richard III

William Shakespeare
Sonnets

William Shakespeare
The Taming of the Shrew

William Shakespeare
Twelfth Night

William Shakespeare
The Winter's Tale

George Bernard Shaw
Arms and the Man

George Bernard Shaw
Saint Joan

Muriel Spark
The Prime of Miss Jean Brodie

John Steinbeck
The Grapes of Wrath

John Steinbeck
The Pearl

Tom Stoppard
Arcadia

Tom Stoppard
Rosencrantz and Guildenstern are Dead

Jonathan Swift
Gulliver's Travels and The Modest Proposal

Alfred, Lord Tennyson
Selected Poems

W.M. Thackeray
Vanity Fair

Virgil
The Aeneid

Edith Wharton
The Age of Innocence

Tennessee Williams
Cat on a Hot Tin Roof

Tennessee Williams
The Glass Menagerie

Virginia Woolf
Mrs Dalloway

Virginia Woolf
To the Lighthouse

William Wordsworth
Selected Poems

Metaphysical Poets

York Notes – the Ultimate Literature Guides

York Notes are recognised as the best literature study guides.
If you have enjoyed using this book and have found it useful, you
can now order others directly from us – simply follow the ordering
instructions below.

HOW TO ORDER

Decide which title(s) you require and then order in one of the following
ways:

Booksellers
All titles available from good bookstores.

By post
List the title(s) you require in the space provided overleaf,
select your method of payment, complete your name and
address details and return your completed order form and
payment to:

>*Addison Wesley Longman Ltd*
>*PO BOX 88*
>*Harlow*
>*Essex CM19 5SR*

By phone
Call our Customer Information Centre on 01279 623923 to
place your order, quoting mail number: HEYN1.

By fax
Complete the order form overleaf, ensuring you fill in your
name and address details and method of payment, and fax it
to us on 01279 414130.

By e-mail
E-mail your order to us on awlhe.orders@awl.co.uk listing
title(s) and quantity required and providing full name and
address details as requested overleaf. Please quote mail
number: HEYN1. Please do not send credit card details by
e-mail.

York Notes Order Form

Titles required:

Quantity	Title/ISBN	Price

Sub total _____

Please add £2.50 postage & packing _____

(*P & P is free for orders over £50*) _____

Total _____

Mail no: HEYN1

Your Name _____

Your Address _____

_____

Postcode _____ Telephone _____

Method of payment

☐ I enclose a cheque or a P/O for £_____ made payable to Addison Wesley Longman Ltd

☐ Please charge my Visa/Access/AMEX/Diners Club card
Number _____ Expiry Date _____
Signature _____ Date _____

(please ensure that the address given above is the same as for your credit card)

Prices and other details are correct at time of going to press but may change without notice. All orders are subject to status.

☐ *Please tick this box if you would like a complete listing of Longman Study Guides (suitable for GCSE and A-level students)*

York Press

Longman

Addison Wesley Longman